AMERICAN PLACE PUZZLERS

Grand and Busy

What Am I?

by Joyce Markovics

Consultant: Eric Darton, Adjunct Faculty
New York University Urban Design and Architecture Studies Program
New York, New York

BEARPORT PUBLISHING

New York, New York

Credits

Cover, © DW labs Incorporated/Shutterstock; 2, © Helen Sessions/Alamy; TOC, © Nigel Spiers/Alamy; 4–5, © Jessicakrish/Shutterstock; 6–7, © redswept/Shutterstock; 8–9, © Nigel Spiers/Alamy; 10–11, © Helen Sessions/Alamy; 12–13, © Bert Broer/Shutterstock; 14–15, © Alpegor/Dreamstime; 16–17, © Joseph Reid/Alamy; 18–19, © Gavin Rogers/Alamy; 20–21, © Gavin Rogers/Alamy; 22, © Bailey-Cooper Photography/Alamy; 23, © RosalreneBetancourt 12/Alamy; 24, © Colin D. Young/Shutterstock.

Publisher: Kenn Goin
Senior Editor: Joyce Tavolacci
Creative Director: Spencer Brinker
Design: Debrah Kaiser
Photo Researcher: Thomas Persano

Library of Congress Cataloging-in-Publication Data

Names: Markovics, Joyce L., author.
Title: Grand and busy : what am I? / by Joyce Markovics.
Description: New York : Bearport Publishing Company, Inc., 2018. | Series: American place puzzlers | Includes bibliographical references and index. |
Identifiers: LCCN 2017039491 (print) | LCCN 2017041995 (ebook) | ISBN 9781684025428 (ebook) | ISBN 9781684024841 (library)
Subjects: LCSH: Grand Central Terminal (New York, N.Y.)—Juvenile literature. | New York (N.Y.)—Buildings, structures, etc.—Juvenile literature. | Manhattan (New York, N.Y.)—Buildings, structures, etc.—Juvenile literature.
Classification: LCC TF302.N7 (ebook) | LCC TF302.N7 M37 2018 (print) | DDC 385.3/14097471—dc23
LC record available at https://lccn.loc.gov/2017039491

For more information, write to Bearport Publishing Company, Inc., 45 West 21st Street, Suite 3B, New York, New York 10010. Printed in the United States of America.

10 9 8 7 6 5 4 3 2 1

Contents

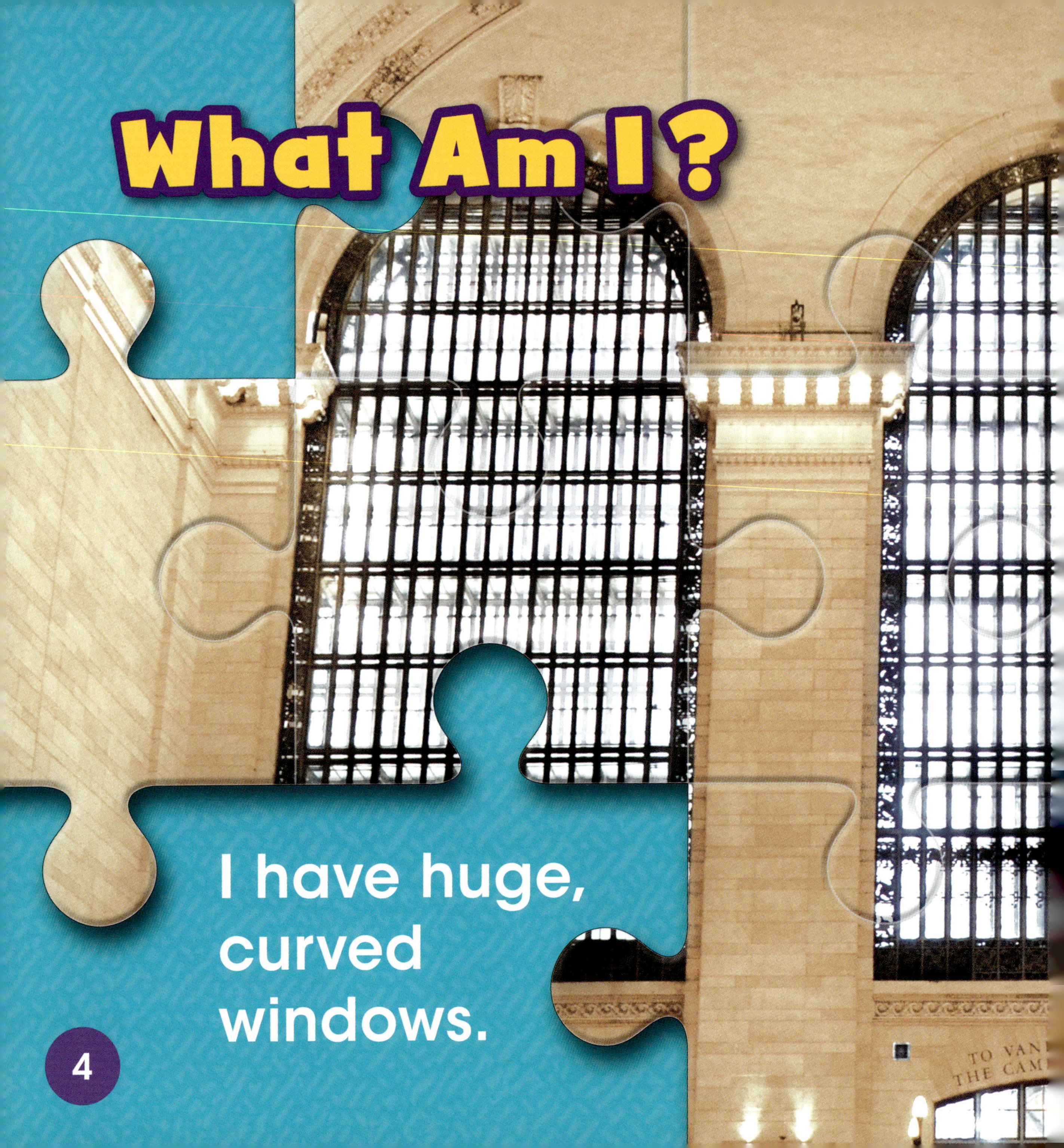

What Am I?

I have huge, curved windows.

Look up!

My ceiling looks like a starry sky.

There is a huge sculpture on my roof.

Tick-tock.
Tick-tock.

I have a clock
with four sides.

A huge board hangs in my main hall.

It gives information to travelers.

Trains move inside me.

30

I am one of the busiest places in the world!

LAINS - 1ST STOP
- 1ST STOP

What am I?

Let's find out!

I am Grand Central Terminal!

CENTRAL
DIRECTORY

Fast Facts

Grand Central Terminal is the largest railroad station in the world. It's also one of the most famous buildings in America.

Grand Central Terminal

Height of Building:	130 feet (39.6 m)
Number of Train Platforms:	44
Number of Train Tracks:	67
Date Terminal Opened:	1913
Cool Fact:	More than 750,000 people visit Grand Central Terminal each day.

Where Am I?

Grand Central Terminal is located in Midtown Manhattan in New York City.

Every day, thousands of people visit shops at Grand Central Terminal.

Index

Read More

Mansfield, Andy. *Pop-Up New York.* New York: Lonely Planet (2016).

Melmed, Laura Krauss, and Frane Lessac. *New York, New York: The Big Apple from A to Z.* New York: HarperCollins (2008).

Learn More Online

To learn more about Grand Central Terminal, visit **www.bearportpublishing.com/AmericanPlacePuzzlers**

About the Author

Joyce Markovics lives in a very old house along the Hudson River. Every day, she makes her way through the grandest train station in the world.